FUTURE ENGINEERING:
THE CLEAN WATER CHALLENGE

Judith Love Cohen
and
Robyn C. Friend

Edited by Lee Rathbone

Cascade
Pass, Inc.
www.cascadepss.com

Copyright © 2015 by Cascade Pass, Inc.
Published by Cascade Pass, Inc.
4223 Glencoe Avenue, Suite C-105
Marina del Rey CA 90292-8801
Phone: (310) 305-0210
Printed in the United States by RR Donnelley

First Edition 2015

Future Engineering: The Clean Water Challenge was written by Robyn C. Friend and Judith Love Cohen, and edited by Lee Rathbone. Book designed and illustrated by David Katz.

This book is one of a series that explains the grand challenges to future engineers as outlined by the National Academy of Engineers and what our future generation can do to meet these challenges.
This is the first book in the series.

Library of Congress Cataloging-in-Publication Data
Friend, Robyn C., 1955-
    Future engineering : the clean water challenge / Robyn C. Friend and Judith Love Cohen ; edited by Lee Rathbone.
        pages cm
        ISBN 978-1-935999-08-9 (pbk.)
        1. Water-supply–Juvenile literature. 2. Water quality management–Juvenile literature.
I. Cohen, Judith Love, 1933- II. Rathbone, Lee. III. Title.

TD348.F75 2015
628.1–dc23   2014043065

Introduction

Water is essential to life on Planet Earth. When we look around our homes and our neighborhoods, water or evidence of water is all around us. The grass, the flowers, the trees, the puddles in the streets, the food—all need water to exist and grow. Even our bodies are 65 percent water!

Most of the time we don't even think about water and where it comes from. We turn on the faucet or the hose and there it is. "It's abundant and it's free!" we think, if we think of it at all.

But in some places in the world getting clean water is not so easy. Even if we see water in the ocean or in a lake, is it clean enough for us to drink or even to wash clothes or bathe in? The poet Samuel Taylor Coleridge once described such a situation by writing, "Water, water, everywhere, nor any drop to drink." And as our climate continues to change, in the future finding clean water may become more difficult.

In this book, we learn about the water cycle and how it presents us with challenges now and in the future. We learn about what people are doing around the world to get access to clean water and what we can do to ensure that we will have clean water in the future.

The Water Cycle

When it rains, water comes down from the clouds and makes puddles on the ground and over time makes its way to oceans, lakes, and rivers. Then the sun comes out, the day gets warm, and the water puddled in the front yard dries up. It *evaporates*. That means that the liquid water turns to *water vapor*, or steam, and becomes part of the clouds in the sky where all the other water drops end up. The clouds get thicker and heavier and finally rain comes and the water drops all fall back down to the ground. The process of water evaporating up to form clouds, and eventually *precipitating* in the form of rain or snow, is called the water cycle.

The water cycle is different in different places on Earth. In some places, the water that dried up will fall back down in the same place and refill the lake or add to the river or ocean where it came from. In other places, snow or rain falls in the mountains, and that water will flow down as streams and rivers when the snow melts or the rain falls. In some areas, however, like deserts, the water dries up, and the clouds form, but the rain falls in some other place, and the land just gets drier.

For thousands of years people have tried to figure out how to move water from the places where it is abundant to the places where it is dry. When we look for sources of water, we must understand the water cycle so we know where water comes from and how to get it.

Water Cycle

Cloud

Cloud

3

Rain

Lake

Ocean

Water Sources

What do you do when you want a drink of water? You just go to the sink and turn on the faucet. You can enjoy your water knowing that it is clean and safe to drink.

But what if you live where there is no plumbing at your house bringing clean, safe water to your faucet?

All around the world, and throughout most of human existence, people have had to get water outside their home. In fact today in Sub-Saharan Africa more than eight out of ten people must get water outside their homes. How do they do that?

One of the most common sources of water is *surface water*. This means water that is sitting right out in the open, like a lake, river or spring. In places where there is a lot of surface water, you can get water easily from a nearby lake or stream. All you have to do is bring your bucket or goatskin bag and scoop up the water.

If there aren't any lakes or streams nearby, you might have to dig a well and bring water up from inside the earth where it collects in pockets underground, called *aquifers*. This is called *groundwater*.

Whether people get their water from surface water or groundwater sources, they often face problems. People in many parts of the world spend a large part of their day collecting water and carrying it back home. In Africa, many people, mostly young girls and women, spend hours each day collecting water and carrying it home in heavy buckets.

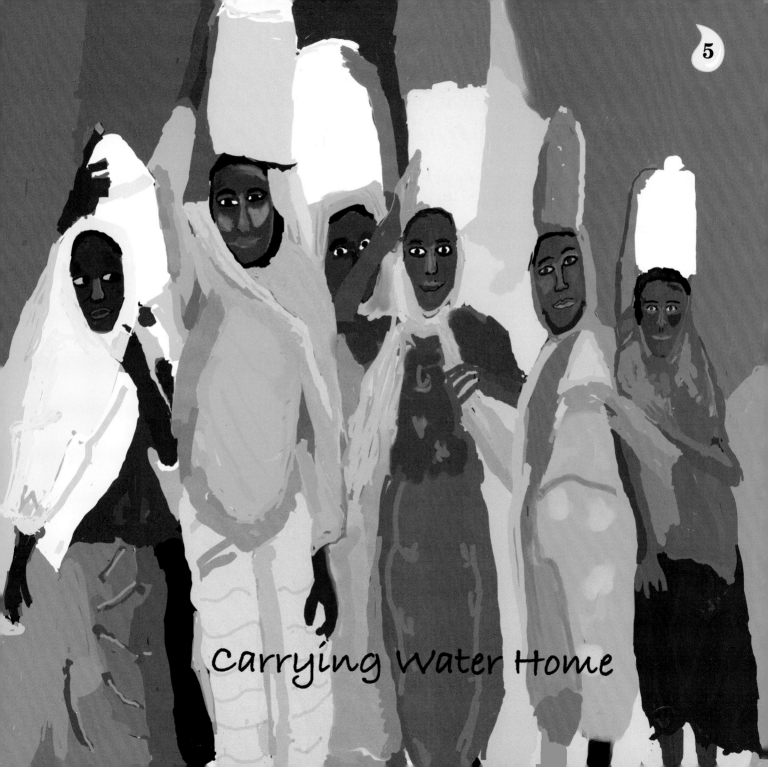

Carrying Water Home

Once the water has been brought to the home, whether from surface water or groundwater sources, it can't necessarily be consumed immediately. Bacteria can grow in the water and other things that we shouldn't be drinking could be dissolved in the water like metal particles or poisons from manufacturing, such as arsenic or mercury. In Africa, for example, children often get diarrhea from bacteria in the water.

The water can be treated in various ways to make it safe to drink. Adding chlorine can kill the bacteria, or the water can be boiled. The water can be filtered to remove metals and other *toxins*.

But you have to know how much chlorine to add to the water, or that also can make you sick. You need to know how long to boil the water to kill the bacteria (15 minutes).

Over human history, though people have invented ways to get water, they haven't always known how to make it safe to drink. Organizations like the U. S. Agency for International Development and companies like Tetra Tech provide assistance to people who live in places where they don't have access to clean water. They train the people in ways to purify the water and help them to improve water systems to bring safe drinking water to their homes.

Sometimes water is abundant in the mountains, where it is too high or rocky for people to live and grow food or raise their animals. In this case, the water must be channeled from the source to where the people need it. In ancient times, the Romans used an invention called the *aqueduct* to bring water to cities, towns, and farms.

Now that we know how people in other times and other places get their water, let's look at some more modern ways of getting clean, safe water to people, including to your faucet!

At your house, you turn on the faucet and the water just comes out. But that water may have come from hundreds of miles away, where a lake or a river is filled by rain or melting snow. In this case, an aqueduct carries the water from the source to you. Along the way, various methods are used to purify the water: water treatment systems, filtration systems, and pumps.

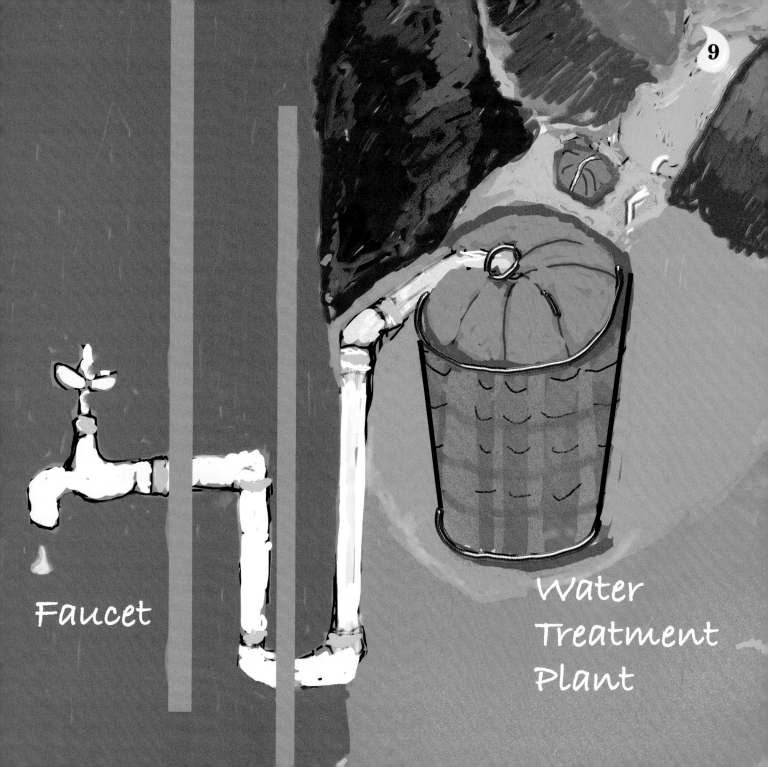

Even in places where there is a lot of local water in wells or streams, the water may be diverted into pipes to treatment areas where it is purified. Then the water is pumped through more pipes to your home, where finally it comes out of a faucet. Your water might also be pumped from groundwater aquifers, but it still goes through the process of purification, so it's safe for you to drink.

It takes a lot of careful planning and training to make sure that these systems are well maintained and that there is enough water to meet all of our needs.

Water from Aquifers

Artesian Wells

Soil Bed

Aquifer

Soil Bed

Water Uses

Water that comes from a long way has many other users along its path to you, and many people, animals, and plants might need to have some of that water. How to allocate the water is a challenge.

Once a *dam* is built to control the flow of water, it creates a big basin of water like a lake, which is called a *reservoir*.

People like to fish and swim in lakes and reservoirs, and float in boats in the water. So there should always be enough water in the reservoir for these activities.

Man Fishing
on Lake

13

The dam not only holds the water back to create sources for drinking water, or to protect communities from floods, but dams also can be used as a power source. Once there is enough water in the reservoir, it can flow through *hydroelectric turbines* to create electric power. Wires then carry the electric power to people's homes and businesses.

Once the water is through the turbines, it keeps flowing down the river to places where it can be used for other purposes, like *agriculture* and drinking water. Along the way, plants and animals that live in and near the river need to be able to get water, too.

Water Flowing Through Hydroelectric Turbines

Farmers use the water to *irrigate* their crops and provide water for their livestock. But they can't use it all up; some still needs to flow farther downstream to where people must be able to use it for drinking, cooking, washing, and gardening.

And these people can't use up all of the water, either; they still need to leave some for plants and animals that live in the *estuary*, the place where the river empties into the sea.

Many estuaries are home to fish and shellfish that people depend on for food.

Lake Bed
Showing Mud

The Future

As our population grows and as more people live in cities, we need more and more water for drinking and other uses. At the same time, weather patterns are changing and some areas will be receiving less rain than they do now. This means that in the future there will be less water available to our cities.

Our challenge is to find ways to use the water we have more efficiently and create new sources of drinking water.

Many cities are asking their citizens to take action to reduce their water usage, by limiting plant watering, taking shorter showers, and making sure the dishwasher or washing machine is full before using. Some cities are encouraging residents to catch rainwater on their properties and use it to water their gardens instead of relying only on distant sources of water.

Can you think of other ways to lower water usage?

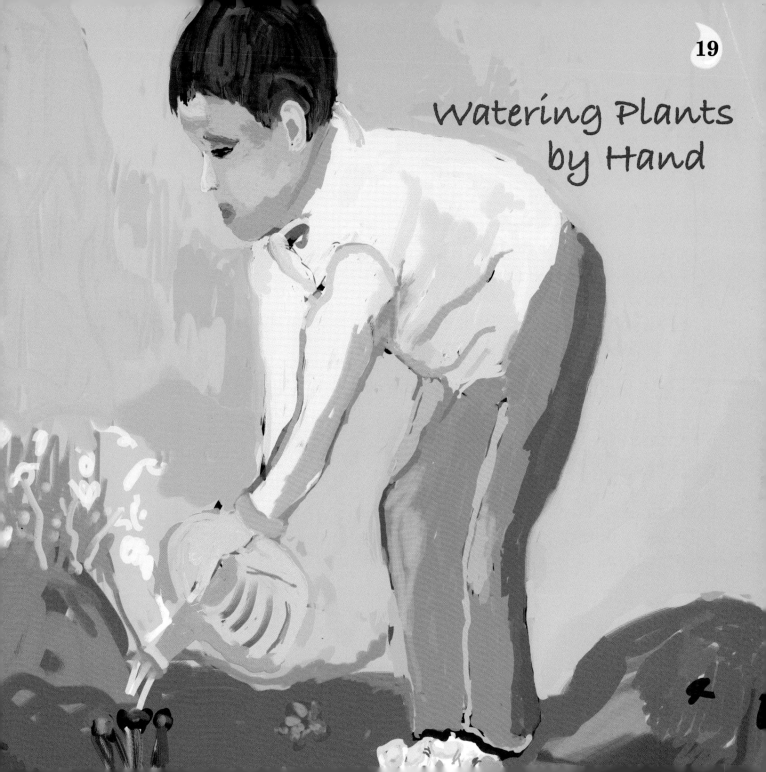

Watering Plants by Hand

In most homes, only a very small amount of water is used for drinking and personal use. Most of it goes down the drain and into the sewer pipes and is sent to the rivers and eventually ends up in the ocean where it can't be used again for drinking. What if we captured that water, treated it and reinjected it into the groundwater aquifer so it could be used again and again?

The technologies for doing this recycling are being developed and used by companies like Tetra Tech in California, Florida and Texas.

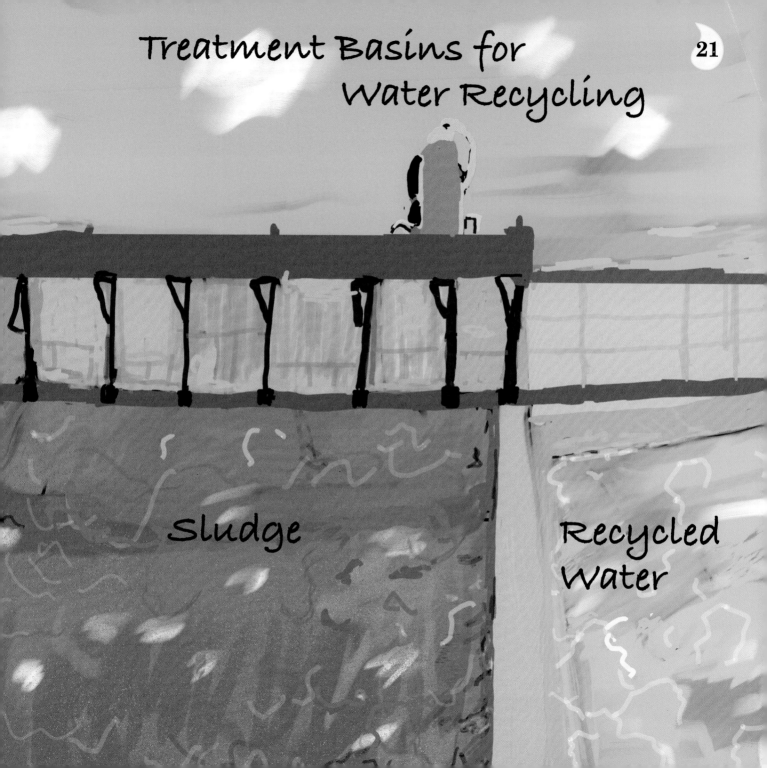

Treatment Basins for Water Recycling

Sludge

Recycled Water

Most of the world's water is in the oceans. But the water in the oceans is too salty for us to use for drinking or bathing or watering plants.

There is a process called *desalination*, which means taking the salt out of the water. Desalination is not new; there are many places in the world with facilities that do it, mostly in places in the Middle East like Saudi Arabia and Israel, where there are few sources of fresh water.

Salty ocean water is pushed at high pressure through a membrane that separates the salt from the water, like a strainer. The challenge is that the process of extracting the salt from seawater uses a lot of energy, which makes it expensive to produce.

New techniques are being developed that use less energy and are just as effective. Tetra Tech helped design a desalination plant in San Diego County that uses new techniques to push the water through the membrane. These techniques save energy and are therefore less expensive to use.

In the future we will need to develop even more technologies to lower the energy needed to create fresh water from seawater. New filters and other ways to improve the process will allow us to get more water from the oceans, especially in less-developed countries where there is a huge demand for access to clean water.

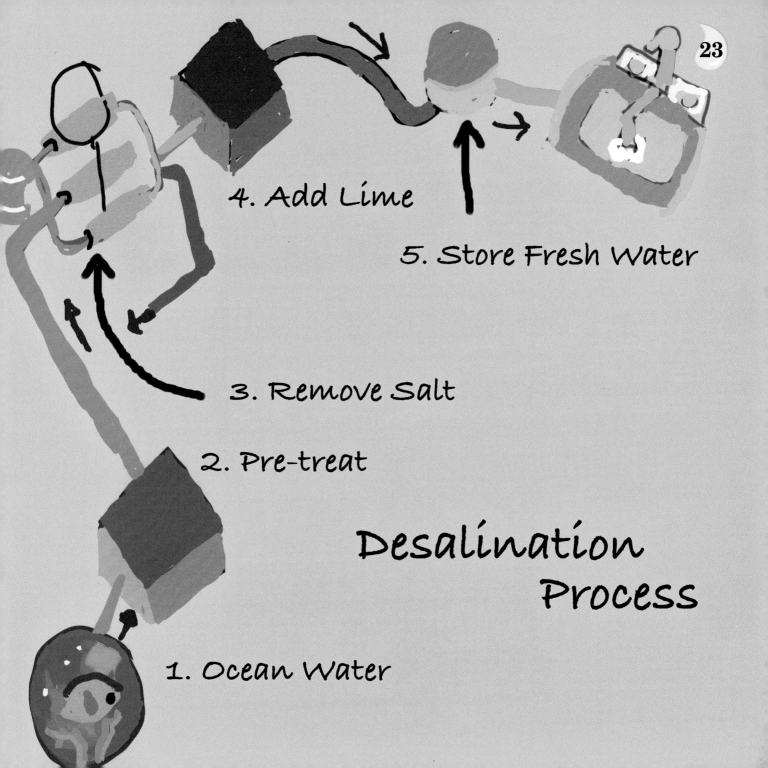

4. Add Lime

5. Store Fresh Water

3. Remove Salt

2. Pre-treat

Desalination Process

1. Ocean Water

Another new way to capture and hold water closer to where people need it is called *green infrastructure*. Cities are made mostly of concrete and asphalt. Water that falls as rain doesn't go into the ground, but washes off into storm drains and eventually gets channeled out to sea. A recent trend in city planning is to build small parks all over the city, with lots of trees, flowers, and other plants. When it rains, the water soaks into the soil and helps to fill up the groundwater aquifers. The trees provide oxygen and cool the air by absorbing sunlight rather than reflecting it back to their surroundings. These *pocket parks* also provide *habitat* for animals and a soothing place for people to enjoy a little bit of nature.

People, plants, and animals all must get the water they need and still leave enough water for all the other uses, too, such as boat navigation and power generation. The weather varies from year to year, yet we need to provide water whether the climate is hot and dry this year, or there is a lot of rainfall and melting snow to supply ample water for everyone.

So how can we know how much water people need and how it can be supplied? One way is by using computer models to look at weather patterns, population, and land use. Scientists put different kinds of data about climate and weather into the model–like the amount of rain, the temperature, and how many people use the water. The models can help them predict how much water would be available and how much water would be needed under various conditions. Then scientists and government can work together to plan better for the future water needs of all.

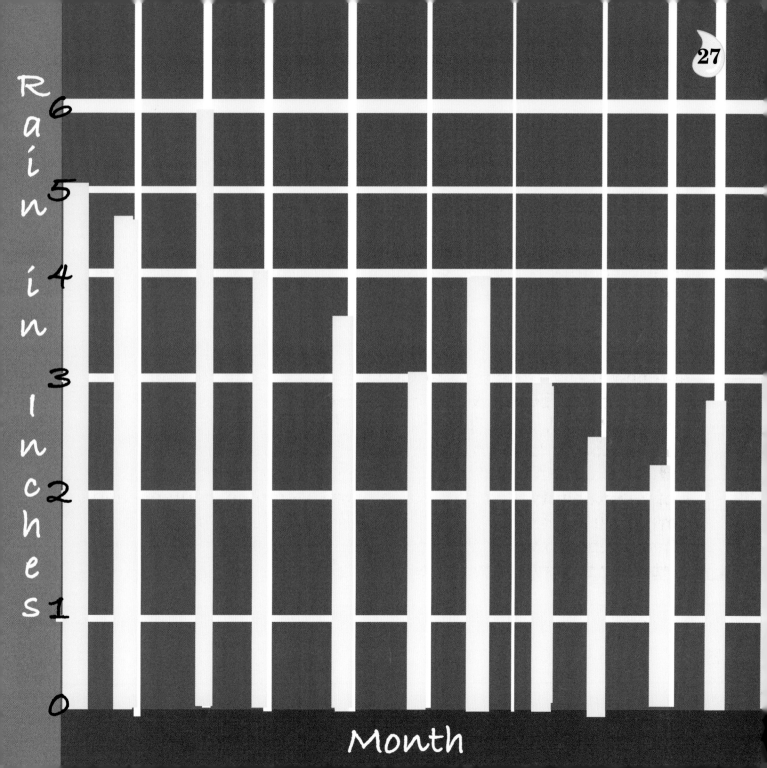

You Can Help!

Making sure everyone has the water they need is a complex but important problem, and you can help. You can start by learning more about your own drinking water and where it comes from: from a river, a reservoir, a well, or from desalinized sea water. When you understand how much effort goes into bringing that glass of water to your kitchen faucet, you will appreciate it more and work harder to *conserve* it. You can do your part by becoming aware of how you use water, and deciding if there are ways that you could use less water. You could do this by taking shorter showers; turning off the tap when you're brushing your teeth; sweeping your driveway rather than hosing it down; and using plants in your yard that don't need a lot of water.

Can you think of other ways to conserve water?

Be a part of the future. Careers to help!

One of the best things you can do to help ensure future clean water for your community and the planet is to become a scientist, learn how the water cycle works and then use that knowledge to discover better ways of water conservation and delivery. By studying mathematics, engineering, and sciences like *chemistry*, *geology*, and *biology*, you can help the people, plants, and animals of the future get the water they need to thrive!

Here are some of the careers you might pursue:

Hydrologist:

A hydrologist studies the movement, distribution, and quality of water on Earth including the water cycle and water resources. A hydrologist works within the fields of earth or environmental science, physical geography, geology, or civil and environmental engineering.

Civil Engineer:

Civil engineering uses mathematics and physics along with the study of different kinds of materials to design structures that are of benefit to people. As a civil engineer, you could plan, design, build, maintain, or operate dams and channels for bringing water from higher elevations down to cities.

Geotechnical Engineer:

Geotechnical engineering is a kind of civil engineering that looks at how earth materials behave. As a geotechnical engineer, you design better ways of getting water from underground.

Chemical Engineer:

Chemical engineers use their knowledge of chemistry to discover new ways to convert raw materials into more useful substances. As a chemical engineer, you could discover newer, less expensive ways to purify water for drinking, or get the salt out of sea water so it can be used for drinking and other uses.

Environmental Engineer:

Environmental engineering combines sciences like mathematics and physics with life sciences like chemistry and biology. As an environmental engineer, you could invent new ways to remove all kinds of pollution, like chemicals from agriculture or city streets.

Computer Scientist:

Computer science uses computers as a way to study large amounts of data. As a computer scientist, you could design improved computer models that more accurately predict future water needs.

Water by the Numbers

Read the questions below to understand how much water we use each day and how many people in the world don't have access to clean water. Then ask your friends and family to guess the answers.

Did you know you can save 8 gallons of water each day by turning off the faucet when you brush your teeth?

Did you know that in the United States we use 400,000,000,000 gallons of fresh water EVERY day?

Did you know that a faucet that drips at one drip per second will waste 3,000 gallons of water a year?

Did you know that more than 750,000,000 people in the world do not have access to clean water?

Did you know that only 2.5 percent of the world's fresh water is available for consumption (the rest is frozen or in the oceans)?

GLOSSARY

Agriculture: The cultivation of animals, plants, fungi, and other life forms for food, fiber, biofuel, medicines and other products; also called farming.

Aqueduct: A type of bridge or large pipe or canal that is constructed to carry water over an obstacle, such as a ravine or valley.

Aquifer: An underground layer of water-bearing rock or materials such as gravel, sand, or silt from which groundwater can be extracted.

Chemical engineering: A branch of engineering that uses science and mathematics to produce and transform chemicals for multiple uses.

Chemistry: A science that deals with the structure and properties of substances and the changes they go through.

Cistern: An enclosed and waterproof vessel for storing water, usually rainwater. It can store a small amount of water (a few liters) or a massive amount, like a reservoir. It is different from a reservoir in that it is completely covered.

Civil engineering: A professional engineering discipline that deals with the design, construction, and maintenance of the physical and natural environment, including roads, bridges, canals, dams and buildings.

Climatology: The study of climate, scientifically defined as weather conditions averaged over a period.

Computer science: The branch of science that deals with the theory and methods of processing information in digital computers, the design of computer hardware and software, and the applications of computers.

Conservation: The act of preserving, guarding or protecting the natural environment.

Dam: A barrier built to hold back water or underground streams.

Desalination: Processes that remove some amount of salt and other minerals from water.

Environmental engineering: A type of engineering that uses both science and engineering to improve the natural environment.

Environmental science: An academic field that combines physical, biological and information sciences to the study of the environment and the solution of environmental problems.

Estuary: The part of the mouth of a river where the river's current meets the ocean's tides.

Evaporation: The natural process of turning a liquid into a gas, such as when heat turns liquid water into water vapor.

Geology: A science that studies rocks, layers of soil, etc., to understand the history of the Earth and its life.

Geotechnical engineering: The branch of civil engineering that deals with the behavior of Earth materials.

Green infrastructure: A way to use vegetation, soils, and natural processes to manage water and create healthier urban environments.

Groundwater: The water under the surface of the ground, consisting of surface water that has seeped down, which is the source of water in springs and wells.

Habitat: An ecological or environmental area that is the home of a particular kind of animal or plant.

Hydroelectric turbines: A kind of engine that takes energy from the movement of water flowing over it and causing it to turn, and converts it to electrical energy.

Hydrology: The study of water on Earth: where it is, how it moves, the quality of it, and the water cycle.

Irrigation: A way of providing water for plants, especially agriculture, by other than natural means, via a hose, canal, etc.

Physical geography: The study of the physical systems of the natural environment.

Physics: The study of matter and motion through space and time.

Pocket park: A small public garden or park in a city, usually created on an area of ground too small for other uses, that adds greenery and a bit of nature to an otherwise completely urban scene.

Precipitation: When water vapor condenses and falls in the form of liquid water (rain) or frozen water (snow, hail, sleet, etc).

Reservoir: A natural or man-made body of water, such as a lake or storage pond. It can be created by digging a hole to catch and hold rainwater or by building a dam to catch and hold water that comes from a river or stream.

Surface water: Water on the surface of the Earth, such as rivers, lakes, streams, and oceans.

Toxins: Poisonous substances produced within living cells or organisms.

Wastewater: Water that has been contaminated in some way by human processes; examples are sewage, urban runoff, and industrial waste.

Water cycle: The continuous movement of water on, above, or below the surface of the Earth.

Water vapor: Water in its gaseous form.

FUTURE ENGINEERING: THE CLEAN WATER CHALLENGE

LESSON PLAN 1

PURPOSE:	To begin to understand how we use water in our daily lives and how we can learn to use less of it.
MATERIALS:	Cards with activities on it that use water: e.g. watering plants, washing your bike, washing the family car, washing dishes, brushing your teeth, washing your body.
PROCEDURES:	Have the children put the cards with activities on them face down on a table. Have each child in turn pick a card and study it. Have each child come up in front of the group and pantomime the activity in an intensive water use way. Have the group try to guess the activity. Then have the child redo a pantomime of the activity in a water conserving way. Have the children write a list as each child does their activities.
CONCLUSIONS:	In what ways do we use too much water at my house? How can I help to change what we do?

LESSON PLAN 2

PURPOSE: To understand where the water at our homes comes from.

MATERIALS: Scissors, glue, shoe boxes, art supplies (paper, crayons, paints, and colored pencils).

PROCEDURES: Have the children use resources below to figure out where the water in their homes comes from.
Have them list what water body it comes from and what it passes on the way to them.
Have children take the shoe box and create an area that will contain the watershed, the rivers, the processing plants, the local distribution, etc., or if it is so, a well or local water body.

CONCLUSIONS: Where does our water come from?
What does it go through to get to us?

RESOURCES: Pictures of the origins of the local water from magazines or the internet. Pictures of structures along the way.

ABOUT THE CONTRIBUTORS:

Tetra Tech's scientists and engineers contributed to the stories in this book. They are developing solutions for some of the world's most complex water projects. Tetra Tech is designing ways to recycle water for new uses in southern California, providing access to drinking water sources in remote regions in western Africa, and improving the quality of water going into our rivers and streams using vegetation and natural materials.

ABOUT THE AUTHORS:

Robyn C. Friend, author, is a singer, dancer, choreographer, and writer. She earned a Ph.D. in Iranian Linguistics at University of California, Los Angeles, and promptly launched a twenty-year career building spacecraft. She has written for both scholarly and popular publications on a wide variety of subjects, including folkloric dance, world music, linguistics, travel, and the exploration of Mars by balloon.

Judith Love Cohen, author, is a Registered Professional Electrical Engineer with bachelor's and master's degrees in engineering from the University of Southern California and University of California, Los Angeles. She has written plays, screenplays, and newspaper articles in addition to her series of children's books that began with *You Can Be a Woman Engineer*.

ABOUT THE ILLUSTRATOR:

David Arthur Katz, art director, received his training in art education and holds a master's degree from the University of South Florida. He is a credentialed teacher in the Los Angeles Unified School District. His involvement in the arts has encompassed animation, illustration, playwriting, poetry, and songwriting.

ACKNOWLEDGEMENTS

Graphic materials created by **Kana Tatekawa**, Tatekawa and Associates.

am.
tw